Successful
Planning for
Retirement
in a week

Malcolm Peel

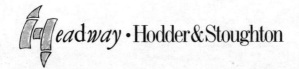

ACKNOWLEDGEMENT

I would like to say thank you publicly to my wife, Nancy, for her thorough reading of the draft, and her perceptive and helpful comments on it.

Cataloguing in Publication Data is available from the British Library

ISBN 0 340 67922 0

First published 1997

Impression number	10	9	8	7	6	5	4	3	2	1
Year	1999		1998		1997					

Typeset by Multiplex Techniques Ltd, St Mary Cray, Kent. Printed in Great Britain for Hodder & Stoughton Educational, a division of Hodder Headline Plc, 338 Euston Road, London NW1 3BH by Cox & Wyman Ltd, Reading.

the Institute of Management

F O U N D A T I O N

The Institute of Management (IM) is at the forefront of management development and best management practice. The Institute embraces all levels of management from students to chief executives. It provides a unique portfolio of services for all managers, enabling them to develop skills and achieve management excellence.

For information on the benefits of membership, please contact:

Department HS
Institute of Management
Cottingham Road
Corby
Northants NN17 1TT
Tel: 01536 204222
Fax: 01536 201651

This series is commissioned by the Institute of Management Foundation.

C O N T E N T S

Retirement can be the Greatest Adventure in life, or the Worst Disaster. Which, will depend largely on the frame of mind in which we approach it. Do we see it more as an end or a beginning? Is it fuller of dangers or of opportunities?

Retirement certainly offers both dangers and opportunities. It may present financial difficulties, social isolation, partnership problems and loss of personal identity. The opportunities include self-determination, freedom from stress, residence in a favourite location, new leisure interests, and more time with one's partner and friends.

Retirement is a time for active choices and informed decisions. However, if we wait until retirement actually happens before making these, the chances of success are less. It is this long-term planning for retirement which is the subject of this book.

Throughout, you are invited to apply what is discussed to your own situation and to build up your own Action Plan. Each main subject will take a day of the week:

Sunday	–	The dangers and opportunities of retirement
Monday	–	Money matters
Tuesday	–	Relationships, residence and the home front
Wednesday	–	Using time (1): time in retirement and earning activities
Thursday	–	Using time (2): community and leisure activities
Friday	–	Fitness and health
Saturday	–	Piecing it all together

The dangers and opportunities of retirement

Retirement has been called 'the greatest killer'. Today, we will look retirement in the face, identifying how we can prove this saying to be absolute nonsense in our case . We will consider:

- The drawbacks and dangers of retirement
- The benefits and opportunities of retirement
- Action planning for retirement

The drawbacks and dangers of retirement

The change from full-time employment is one of the most traumatic events in many people's lives. Its effects can be comparable with marriage, divorce, the birth of a child, serious injury or illness, or the death of a partner. Damage from a traumatic event is usually greatest when the event is unexpected, for example, sudden death, accident, or the unanticipated break-up of a relationship. In the past, retirement was rarely unexpected; its date was foreseeable from the start of our working life. Recently, however, this has become far less certain. Retirement has been forced on many without warning.

However it comes, retirement will bring problems of adjustment as we seek to fit ourselves into a completely different world. There is nothing to be gained by trying to deceive ourselves or ignoring what we know to be real difficulties. As with all traumas, the way forward starts by facing the facts.

For this reason, we will begin the week by facing fears about retirement. We will look briefly at the following aspects:

- Retirement and ageing
- Loss of self-respect
- Loss of job satisfaction
- Loss of companionship
- Financial problems
- Spending too much time in the home

Retirement and ageing
One of the difficulties many people face as they contemplate forthcoming retirement is the connection and confusion between retirement and ageing.

In the past there was a very close connection. At the start of the twentieth century, when the 'old age pension' was first introduced in the UK, men retired at 65, and the average expectancy of life for men was little more. Those who made it to retirement were likely, on average, to die within 12 months.

Over the last 90 years, this situation has changed fundamentally. The average age of retirement has fallen until it is now less than 60 years for men. At the same time, the average life expectancy has steadily increased, and is now well over 70 years. Men are now thus likely to enjoy 15 to 20 years of life after retirement. Women may, on average, have 25 to 30 years to look forward to.

The term 'the Third Age' has been coined to emphasise the long period of continuing physical and mental vigour now common between retirement and the onset of old age. A similar thought has been expressed by describing people of this age as 'grey panthers'.

Loss of self-respect
Self-respect is often the first casualty of retirement.

We may have a negative picture of others who have retired. The words '(old age) pensioner' or 'senior citizen' may carry a stigma for us. If they do, it will be difficult not to lose self-respect when at last we join the club.

The problem is made worse because retired people, by definition, no longer have a job role to give them a defined place in society. Our 'occupation' is the way we are most clearly placed and anchored in society. When we meet someone new socially, one of our first questions is likely to be, 'What do you do?' If we meet them in a working situation, we will be keen to learn their job title.

Bureaucrats ask for our 'occupation' on their forms. When a son or daughter first mentions a new close friend, we are sure to ask what they (and their parents) do. When we talk to children, we ask 'What do you want to be when you grow up?', meaning 'What job would you like to have?' A key feature of the Action Plan we will develop during this week must be to provide new, equally strong anchors for our self-image.

For these reasons, some people do not describe themselves as 'retired', but use a term that describes their interests or continuing activities, for example 'consultant', 'writer', 'local historian', etc. This is perfectly legitimate, and can do much to preserve our sense of identity, and even enhance it.

Loss of job satisfaction
The satisfaction we get from doing our job and doing it well can be taken for granted, as long as we are employed. The feelings of a sense of purpose, of achievement, of overcoming problems, of satisfying others and ourselves are important elements in our self-image; the sort of person we feel we are. When we retire, these satisfactions may disappear.

There is also the danger that, without the stimulation of continuing job demands, we may find our mental perspectives narrowing and our knowledge becoming obsolescent. We may become out-of-date.

We can, of course, look to the past, and remember our achievements when we were in work. A little of this may help, but looking back is always dangerous. Looking forward is a better approach, especially by setting clear objectives for our retired life (we will return to this theme several times during the week). Continuing self-development will also become more important than ever, and we may have to work harder at it (we will touch on this on Thursday).

Loss of companionship
Work brings people contacts, whatever our job. Day-by-day we meet colleagues, customers, suppliers and fellow-professionals. They write letters to us, ring us up, pop into our office and join us at meetings. They may be of all kinds of people: young and old, male and female, important and lowly. However nicely people talk when we go ('We *must* keep in touch', '*Do* pop in whenever you feel like it', etc), retirement will mean the loss of these contacts. Replacing this companionship can be a difficult task (we will consider this on Wednesday and Thursday).

Financial problems
If our pension arrangements are not as good as we would like, for whatever reasons, loss of income on retirement will be a major concern (we will think about this problem in detail tomorrow).

Spending too much time in the home
A problem which most couples rapidly encounter when one of them retires, is the need to rebuild their relationship. The main breadwinner is likely to have spent much of each day away from the home and the domestic routine will have been in the control of the other partner, unless both are employed full-time. This can bring problems (we will look at these concerns on Tuesday).

The Benefits and opportunities of retirement

The benefits and opportunities of retirement are many.
They include the following:

- Absence of work stresses and freedom from the demands and instructions of superiors
- No more early mornings, commuting or work travel
- Time for self-development, and possibly gaining additional qualifications
- Following old, and developing new, leisure interests
- Undertaking charitable work or community activities
- Living in a chosen location
- Spending more time with our partner
- Opportunities for travel
- Making new friendships
- Maybe starting a fresh career!

Becoming a new person
Because retirement frees us from the external restraints of
employment, it offers an unrivalled chance to revise and
recast our lifestyle. We can set completely fresh long-term
goals, develop new interests, learn new skills, cultivate new
relationships, live somewhere else. We can become, in
short, a new person. Our thinking this week will be aimed
at helping us to do just that.

Action planning for retirement

It is tempting to leave planning for retirement far too late.
Few people can take such issues as pension provision
seriously during the early years of their career, but this is
exactly the time when such issues should be addressed; a
sensible decision in our twenties may make a crucial
difference to the level of our income forty years later. The
same is true of other aspects of retirement. Have we, for
example, built up interests and friendships during our
career that will serve us after its end? Have we taken care
of our long-term health? Have we taken opportunities to
put down roots in the place we plan to live? All these and
many more preparations are much better considered and
made long before we actually retire – in some cases even at
the very start of our employment, as factors in our career
and job choice.

For the first time, it is all up to us! Happy and successful retirement depends, more than any other phase of life, in deciding what we want in the long and short term, and taking action to achieve it. However, we cannot sensibly do this until we have reviewed each aspect of our retirement situation thoroughly.

Your own position

We are now in a position to begin our retirement planning by building a positive self-image of ourselves in retirement. Here is a simple exercise designed to help us set what we have looked at today into our own context. We will, deliberately, look first at the negative factors – the areas of potential danger. After this, we will bring out the positive factors – the opportunities.

What worries me about retirement
List as many aspects of retirement as possible that worry you, in whatever way. In thinking about this list, consider the kind of factors identified in the first section of this chapter. Do not put something on the list just because you feel you should; only if it really concerns you. Do not omit any factors that you are ashamed of; be totally honest.

Rank the factors to indicate their relative importance to you.

What I look forward to in retirement
List as many aspects of retirement as possible that you look forward to. In thinking about this list, consider the kind of factors identified in the second section of this chapter. Do not put something on the list just because you feel you should; only if it is really true for you. Do not omit any factors because you think of them as self-indulgence, or because they appear too trivial.

Rank the factors to indicate their relative importance to you.

The balance sheet
Compare the two lists carefully, ensuring they do not contain gaps or contradictions. Decide which factors seem more powerful, and what makes them so important. Think about actions which will help to strengthen the positive factors, and eliminate or weaken the negative factors.

During the rest of the week, our aim will be to build up a realistic Action Plan that will enable us to avoid the dangers, while taking maximum advantage from the opportunities.

Summary

- Retirement presents drawbacks and dangers as well as benefits and opportunities
- Retirement planning should begin by facing our own fears honestly. These fears may include loss of self-respect, job satisfaction and companionship, financial problems, and spending too much time at home
- The many benefits of retirement may include reduction of stress from work, commuting and travel, opportunities for self-development, leisure interests, travel and community activities, and living in a chosen location
- Action planning for retirement should begin long before retirement
- Systematic planning should include the elements of finance, residence and the home front, use of time, health and fitness
- A key feature of planning is the setting of short-, medium- and long-term objectives

Money matters

Money is the main concern of many people approaching retirement. Today, we will look at this under the following headings.

- How much will I have (capital)?
- How much will I have (income)?
- What will I need?
- Constructing a realistic budget

How much will I have (Capital)?

Capital is what we possess, expressed in money terms. **Income** is the stream of money coming to us over time. It is, of course, possible to convert income into capital by saving. It is also possible to convert capital into income, either by spending it or by purchasing annuities. However, both these are steps you should take only after careful thought, especially converting capital into income by spending. Living off capital is not a good idea if it can possibly be avoided. Capital may include such items as:

- Bank accounts
- Building society deposits (including TESSAs)
- Stocks and shares
- Unit trusts, etc (including PEPs)
- Life insurance policies
- Residential property
- Marketable possessions

Bank accounts

Unless you keep your spare cash in an old sock under the bed, you are likely to have a bank current account. Current accounts rarely produce interest and may be subject to charges. On approaching retirement, we need to consider (a) how large our average balance should be, and (b) whether we can obtain the services we now need from an interest-bearing account. Approaching retirement should also spur us to examine the standing orders and direct debits against our account – this often produces surprises.

Building society deposits (including TESSAs)

Building society accounts offer the advantages of security, simplicity and ease of withdrawal. Their drawbacks are the lack of capital appreciation and the generally low and variable levels of interest. *TESSAs (Tax-exempt special savings accounts)* provide, as the name implies, tax-free interest, but only when certain conditions are met (in respect of regular contributions and absence of withdrawals) during their five-year term. They may not help in retirement. Many people conclude that building society accounts help to cushion emergencies and unplanned expenditure, but are not suitable for large capital amounts.

Unit trusts (including PEPs)

Despite their spread of risk, Unit Trusts are subject to the fluctuations of the stock markets. Capital invested can thus lose as well as gain value, and the timing of purchase and sale may be critical. Their costs also include the spread between buying and selling price and management fees. For these reasons, they are generally considered only suitable for medium- and long-term investment (typically more than five years) and may not be ideal for new investment on retirement. Despite the benefit of tax exemption, the risks and costs attached to *Personal Equity Plans (PEPs)* are the same as with other unit trusts or shares.

Stocks and shares
The growth of unit trusts has reduced the attraction of direct share ownership for many people with moderate amounts of capital to invest. For those with large amounts of capital, most stockbrokers provide an advisory service for their clients' portfolios, which will take into account their needs and circumstances.

Life insurance policies
The value of life insurance policies (which provide a capital sum on maturity) depends on the value of the underlying investments. *Endowment* policies of this type, used as a means of financing house purchase, may not necessarily be adequate to repay the loan. You must check up on the expected value as their maturity approaches.

Residential property
For many people, the home they live in forms the bulk of their capital. You may already have moved somewhere smaller if your children have left home. If not, retirement may be the trigger for a move, thus releasing a proportion of the capital. Many people will have paid off any mortgage by the time of retirement. This step should in any case always be considered during the last few years of a repayment mortgage, when the tax advantages will be minimal.

Marketable possessions
You may be a conscious collector of antiques, stamps, Wisden's Almanacs or whatever, or by chance, you may have accumulated possessions with a market value. Retirement is a

trigger to assess the current value of these possessions and to decide whether to keep them. If you are planning a move into a smaller home, there may be no room for them. However, if you do consider selling, it may prove difficult to find the right buyer. Dealers rarely offer a fair price. Unless the items are of high interest and you go to a specialised national house, the chances of a worthwhile sale by auction are limited. Advertising in suitable special-interest journals, personal contacts or membership of relevant clubs or societies may offer the best hope.

Other items

While you are likely to have spent a good deal over the years on furniture and household goods, it is unlikely that they will have much value when you have finished with them. It is more probable that you will have to pay someone to take them away. Most people need a car in retirement, but one is usually enough. If you have a company car, you may be forced to dig into your capital to find a replacement. If you have bought any items on hire-purchase or with loans, you will need to consider whether to repay any outstanding loans on or before retirement.

How much will I have (Income)?

The main elements of retirement income may include:

- State retirement pension
- Occupational pension(s)
- Private pension
- Annuities
- Interest
- Payment from continuing employment
- Rents
- Social security payments

State retirement pension
Since the early 1900s, all citizens have, by law, contributed towards a state retirement pension. This is currently payable to males at age 65 and females at age 60. After the year 2020, both will become eligible at age 65; the change will be phased in between the years 2010 and 2020. There may be a gap (10 years or even more) between retirement and eligibility for state pension.

The rules for state pensions are complex. A range of leaflets is issued by the Benefits Agency which may be obtained from Social Security offices. Your entitlement will depend on a number of features, including the number of years of contributions paid. If you cease working before the age of 60, you may not have paid sufficient for a full pension, and it will be necessary to check your position and what action you should take. It is possible to get information on your likely entitlement by completing and submitting DSS Form BR 19.

Occupational pension(s)

Occupational pension schemes are of two sorts: *money purchase* and *final salary*. Under money purchase schemes, the benefits depend on the funds accumulated for each individual, which are used to purchase an annuity on retirement. Final salary schemes provide a level of benefit depending on the final salary level (or possibly the average salary over several years before retirement) and the number of years in the scheme. Many schemes have provision for a lump sum payment, or for the commutation of a proportion of pension into a lump sum.

While it is possible to retire before the normal retirement age set by our employer, the 'actuarial reduction' in pension that will be made is usually great. Early retirement is thus unattractive unless special inducements are offered by the employer.

The European Court of Justice has decided that men and women must have equal rights to join an occupational pension scheme, and pensions earned from service since 17 May 1990 must be equal for both sexes.

Additional Voluntary Contributions (AVCs) up to a maximum of 25% of salary can be made by employees who belong to an occupational pension scheme. Contributions qualify in the same way as standard pension contributions for income tax relief. They can be used only to provide additional pension by the purchase of an annuity. The amount of pension they will eventually provide depends on the value of underlying investments and current interest rates, and cannot be forecast accurately. AVCs do not have to be invested in the same way or with the same pension provider as the employer's main scheme.

Employees who *change* employer may use their
accumulated pension funds from a previous employer to
buy into their new employer's scheme or a private scheme.
Alternatively, they may only take out a proportion of their
accumulated pension funds, or decide to leave the funds
where they are to provide a pension on final retirement.
The decision as to which course to follow may be difficult,
and calls for disinterested professional advice.

All occupational pension schemes are required to give
members annual statements of their current position; we
should read them with care.

Private pensions
Private pensions are not constrained by the age limitations
of an employer's scheme and may legally be drawn at any
age from 50 to 75. Those with such schemes may thus be in
a position to retire early or continue in employment while
drawing a pension. All private pension providers will give
information about the likely level of benefit on request.

However, as with AVCs, this can only be a general indication, and the actual level will depend on the fluctuations of the market and the current interest rates.

Annuities

An *annuity* is a financial arrangement under which a provider contracts to pay an individual a set income for life, beginning at a set age, in return for a once-off payment. The amount of the income will depend on the interest rates available at the time the annuity is purchased, the age of the individual and the age at which annual payments are to begin. It is possible to purchase annuities with built-in escalation (typically 5% per year); however, the starting value of these will be substantially lower than annuities providing a set annual sum. Purchase of an annuity offers the advantage of a fixed and known annual income which will continue as long as you live. It has the disadvantage of a loss of spending control over some of your capital.

Interest

Interest from most **building society and bank accounts** fluctuates, making accurate financial planning difficult. It is wisest to plan on a lower level of interest rather than an optimistic one.

Some **National Savings** schemes pay fixed rates of interest. One scheme, which used to be called 'Granny Bonds' and is correctly known as 'Pensioners Bonds', is specifically designed for those over the age of 60. This provides a regular monthly income at a rate fixed for five years from the date of purchase (on an investment of currently between £500 and £50,000).

Unit trusts designed to produce income will pay higher levels of interest and also offer the possibility of capital growth. However, both the income and capital may go down as well as up.

Income at a fixed rate may be obtained from *government bonds ('gilt-edged securities')*. However, the value of bonds fluctuates to reflect the changing interest rates and the time remaining until they are due for redemption. Thus, if interest rates rise, the market value of the bonds will fall to compensate; if rates fall, the market value of the bonds will rise.

Interest from most forms of investment is paid less UK income tax at the standard rate. We may thus be entitled to a refund. However, this will not be paid until after the end of the tax year.

Apart from considering the level of interest (from whatever source), you need to consider how frequently it is paid; monthly, quarterly or annually.

Payment from continuing employment
There is nothing to stop those who have retired taking up other full - or part-time employment or becoming self-employed. However, in time of heavy unemployment counting on such income will be risky.

Rents
If you move into cheaper accommodation, you may consider renting your old home out. Recent landlord and tenant legislation in the UK has made this more attractive, although risks and costs may make the net income lower than expected.

Social security and other payments and benefits
A range of means-tested benefits may be payable to those receiving a State Retirement Pension whose total incomes are below the respective current thresholds; this includes Income Support, Housing Benefit, Council Tax Benefit, payments from the Social Fund (Funeral Payments, Cold Weather Payments, Community Care Grants and Budgeting and Crisis Loans), free NHS dental treatment, sight tests, glasses, hearing aids and hospital travel costs. Details of all these are available from Social Security offices.

What will I need?

As we saw yesterday, retirement is a time for choices, and these choices will affect our financial planning. We must face decisions on such aspects as:

- What retirement lifestyle do I want?
- The economies of retirement
- What are the risks?
- What do I want to leave for the children?

What retirement lifestyle do I want?

Our lifestyle may be determined by our financial situation, but we usually have some degree of choice. At one end of the scale, we may decide to devote our resources to expensive pleasures: the world cruise, the expensive car, the five-star hotels, the good food and wine. Maybe the spree will not last long, we might say, but while it's there, I intend to get the most out of it. On the other hand, frugality and sober control may attract us: our aim may be to husband our resources for as far into the future as we may.

You may feel the time has come to clarify your *attitude* towards financial risk, and possibly to change it. You may decide that security must be the order of the day, that the time for risks has passed. You might, on the other hand, decide that the time for caution is over, and that with only yourself to please, you can take risks that would have been unthinkable before.

Our attitude to self-sufficiency will also be crucial. Those who believe that the state owes them a duty of care in return for a lifetime of taxes will take a different view from those who value financial independence at any cost. Then again, we may see it as our children's duty to support us in old age, or, alternatively, believe we must do all we can to avoid burdening them.

The economies of retirement
Retirement usually brings some economies. Income will no longer be subject to national insurance and occupational pension contributions. Lower income and (from age 65) the Age Allowance will help reduce the amount of tax. Travel costs will be reduced by the elimination of commuting. Clothing costs will probably be lower, as working clothes will no longer be necessary. Out-of-pocket expenses often fall in a number of intangible ways, perhaps simply because we tend to leave the house less.

If we have reached the age of state pension, we shall also be entitled to a range of perks, such as the Railcard (available to both sexes from age 60), entitling us to reductions in rail fares; bus passes, whose availability and value will depend on local conditions; and concessions on leisure facilities (which may include admission to leisure centres or clubs, concert and theatre seats). It will be worth sinking our pride, if we have any in such matters, and finding out what is available.

What are the risks?
Some financial risks affect the retired more forceably than those in employment.

The annual wage-round acts as a cushion against the effects of **inflation**; in retirement, this cushion is taken away, and inflation will affect both income and expenditure.

The **state pension** is largely inflation proof. However, the annual adjustment is made by comparison with the level of the *Retail Price Index (RPI)* on 1st November each year, and this may or may not be a valid index of overall inflation.

Occupational pensions will be adjusted according to the rules of individual schemes – some generous, some minimal – we need to know how ours is arranged. It is also necessary to bear in mind that scheme rules can be changed.

Interest on fixed investments is calculated (at whatever rate) on the nominal value of the capital sum. Thus, if we have £100 invested in a building society, interest will be calculated on the figure of £100. However, long-term inflation causes the real value of that £100 (its purchasing power) to lessen continuously. The real value of the interest will thus also steadily lessen. How much will depend on the rate of inflation, but at a rate of 5% a year, the purchasing value of money halves in under 14 years.

Interest levels will also rise or fall according to the financial policy of the government of the day, something that is impossible to predict.

Changes in the levels and methods of **taxation** can cause havoc with the best constructed budgets. Income tax levels, thresholds and allowances may affect our disposable income. Changes to indirect taxes (including Value Added Tax, council tax, capital gains tax and inheritance tax) can be even more damaging. It is impossible to anticipate such changes; general prudence is the only defence.

Our likely **health** (and that of our partner), is one of the hardest factors to predict in financial planning. It is critical in three ways: **life expectancy, the costs of health care and long-term disability.**

Life expectancy is the most crucial factor, and also the biggest unknown. Actuaries produce tables of life expectancy from which we may establish, for example, that the life expectancy of a UK male aged 60 is currently 15 years, and of a female of the same age 23 years. But these averages tell us nothing about the date of our own death. If we are fortunate enough to live much longer, this could bring financial difficulties in later years. This is the strongest argument against living off capital in retirement.

The cost of health care will be another unknown. The financial problems will be less if we rely on the National Health Service. We can also take out (or continue) health insurance. However, the rates for those in later life are high, and coverage may not be as comprehensive as we expect.

The need for **long-term residential or continuing home care** is a daunting possibility. Private retirement homes are extremely expensive. Local authority homes may be available, but those entering them will be required to forfeit all assets above £10,000 to pay the costs. We can insure against this risk, but premiums are high, and rise steeply with age. To preserve our capital, we can give assets to children or others. However, the regulations are interpreted with increasing fierceness, and to be effective, such gifts would have to be made (under good legal advice) a long time before the need for care arose.

Some believe that long-term care is a family responsibility. However, this can bring great strain on other members of the family.

Current legislation and medical ethics are implacably set against any form of euthanasia, but some see an advantage in making it clear in advance to family and medical advisers that we do not wish our life to be prolonged in case of terminal illness or total loss of faculties.

What do I want to leave for the children?
Some people take the view that to pass on capital is a major element in family responsibility. Others may feel that adult children must look after themselves, and that they are likely in any case to spend any inheritance quickly and in ways their parents would not approve. As always, the choice must be ours! Many people use retirement as a trigger to review and, if necessary, revise their will.

Constructing a realistic budget – your own position

The process of budgeting has five basic steps. These are:

1 Review capital resources
2 Establish likely income
3 Estimate probable expenditure
4 Plan adjustments
5 Set up contingencies

1 Review capital resources
We should make the best estimate possible of our resources of capital at the expected date of retirement (including any lump sum that we will be entitled to). We should always understate rather than overstate values. The list given at the start of this chapter may help to ensure that nothing is forgotten.

2   Establish likely income

In doing this, we will need to take account of our partner's income and assets (with their full agreement). It is helpful to estimate 'most probable' and 'worst case' figures. We should also indicate those items that are likely to be affected by inflation. We should always make lower estimates rather than higher estimates; this is particularly important when estimating interest. Again, the list near the start of this chapter may help.

3   Estimate probable expenditure

In estimating probable expenditure, prudence suggests that we should err towards higher estimates. All elements will, sadly, be liable to inflation. Here is a checklist to help:

- Food & consumables
- Heat/light/power
- Household maintenance and repairs
- Travel and car (including depreciation)
- Council tax
- Footwear and clothing
- Telephone
- Insurances
- Other

Note There is, deliberately, no provision for holidays and other leisure activities. We can consider them after we see how the essentials stack up!

4   Plan adjustments

If we are in the fortunate position of seeing probable income substantially in excess of expenditure, we can breathe deep sighs of relief. We can also consider

pencilling in amounts for those world cruises and luxury
weekends. However, before doing so, we should:

- Look carefully at those elements of income that are
  likely to lose value from inflation
- Consider whether we have made sensible provision
  for health care in the short and long term

If, before or after these adjustments, likely expenditure is
close to (or even exceeds) probable income, serious thought
will be needed. The possibilities to consider will include:

- Moving to cheaper accommodation and investing
  the capital freed
- Moving capital into higher interest-bearing
  investments
- Realising unnecessary assets (valuable
  possessions, etc)
- Looking for sources of additional income for self or
  partner
- Reducing expenditure (e.g. motoring costs)

5 Set up contingencies
We should not leave the planning process without asking
the following questions.

- What might go wrong?
- How can I: (a) prevent, (b) cope with, or (c) live
  with this potential problem?

In considering these questions, the section in this chapter
'What are the risks' may help to ensure we have covered
everything.

Summary

- Retirement financial planning should include a careful assessment of capital, income and expected needs
- Capital resources may include bank and building society accounts, stocks and shares, unit trusts, life insurance policies, residential property, marketable possessions and other items
- Retirement income may include a state retirement, occupational or private pension; annuities; interest; payment from continuing employment; rents; and social security payments
- Post-retirement financial needs will depend on lifestyle, and will be affected by our attitude to self-sufficiency, the economies of retirement, the desire to leave resources for children, and the expected risks
- The risks affecting financial plans include the levels of inflation and taxation, our health and life expectancy and that of our partner

Relationships, residence and the home front

Today we will consider relationships and home after retirement. We will look at:

- Partnerships and friendships
- To move or not to move?
- Where to move to

Partnerships and friendships

Retirement will affect all our relationships; the more intimate, the more they will be affected. We will need to think about retirement and:

- Our partner
- The rest of the family
- Our friends

Retirement and our partner
Retirement has proved a testing time for many marriages
and partnerships. We suggested on Sunday that, if we have
a partner, retirement planning should be a partnership affair.

If one partner has full-time responsibility for the home, the
two will spend much more time together when the other
retires. This may be unalloyed pleasure for both, but often
it proves to be too much of a good thing. Partners may get
under each other's feet. There will be a temptation for the
retiring partner to make domestic organisation a substitute
for the working role they have lost – and the domestic
partner will not take kindly to being told how to do
housework. They may also expect a re-allocation of house
and garden tasks to take account of the time the retiring
partner can now contribute.

The financial effects of retirement may prove a source of
problems, unless both partners accept the new situation
and the changes it will bring.

The possibility of moving home is also likely to arise, and
will need joint decision making (this is discussed in the
next section).

Even in the most stable relationships, partners need
personal time and space; the retirement of one will make
this harder for both to achieve. Partners may find out
things about each other they had long forgotten, or perhaps
that they never knew.

The relationship will usually need serious re-shaping. If
ever there was a need for frank discussion between
partners, this is it!

Retirement and the rest of the family
All other close members of the family will be affected to some degree by our retirement.

Loneliness, even isolation, is one of the hazards we face. We may suddenly realise just how many relations we have, and remember that we have neglected Cousin Emily shamefully, or failed to reply to Uncle Bean's letters for years. This may lead to happy re-unions, but it may also unearth buried animosities or expose long-hidden family skeletons. We must beware of using the family too much as a substitute for the working companionship we have lost.

The greatest effect is likely to be on our children. If they live with us, they will be involved in any decision about moving home. If they continue with us, we may have to ask for a greater contribution towards household expenses. Children with their own families may look to us for more babysitting time, or they may dread us spending too much of our new-found leisure with them.

Retirement and our friends

Our friends, like our relations, are likely to seem suddenly more precious. We will turn to them also as a substitute for the working companionship we have lost. We may review our friendships, and suddenly realise that we have ignored birthdays and failed to return invitations for far too long. Our new warmth may be welcome, especially to those friends who have also retired. But we may be tempted to rely on some friendships too much, either emotionally or by demanding too much time.

Retirement may provide opportunities to develop new friendships. This will come as a spin-off from new activities, but may result quite simply from having more time to spend getting to know our neighbours and the others we meet. Many a friendship has sprung up, for example, in the aisles of the supermarket.

Holding on too tightly to the friendship of our ex-colleagues can prove a trap. However warm the send-off they give us, and however many the invitations to 'keep in touch', we can easily outstay our welcome. Unless friendships with our colleagues involved non-work contact before we retired, it is unwise to presume that they will stand the separation of retirement.

To move or not to move?

Reasons for moving

Many people choose to move at or near to retirement. For the first time in our life it is no longer necessary to live somewhere that is convenient for our place of work –

commuting has become a thing of the past, and we are *free* to live wherever we want!

This may lead us to follow our dream. For years, we may have yearned to spend our days in that wonderful village we first visited on our honeymoon, to live in a town that has a good football team, or to return to the haunts of our childhood.

We may want to live near our children. Our children may even want us to live near them; if they have families of their own, they may welcome free babysitters and grandparents on whom they can off-load the children.

The motivation to move may be financial. By selling a large or more expensive home and buying one that is smaller and cheaper or is located in an area of lower costs, we can release capital and reduce running costs. If our resources are large, we may consider moving for tax reasons, perhaps to such places as the Isle of Man or the Channel Isles where our liabilities may be lower.

For some, retirement provides the opportunity to make life simpler by finding a home that is easier to run, perhaps one without a garden, with fewer rooms to clean, on one floor and with a labour-saving layout. Although we may still be enjoying full health and vigour, this maybe is the moment when we look ahead to times when it might no longer be so true.

For some, weather is a crucial factor. They dream of luxuriating in sun and warmth throughout the year.

These are all powerful reasons to move. But all too many people move home in haste and live to regret it later, or even move back.

The dangers of moving
Perhaps the most serious dangers of a move on retirement are social. Unless we are moving somewhere we already know well, we will lose friends, neighbours and community involvement. Putting down roots in a new place is always a long-term activity; worthwhile relationships cannot spring up overnight. Unfortunately, some of the locations we may think of as most attractive (particularly rural areas) may be just those in which 'incomers' may be kept at arms' length for longest.

On Sunday we saw how potentially traumatic the change of retirement can be. To move home at the same time may produce serious stress. The move itself can be highly stressful, for example, if we are moving to a smaller home, we shall have to give up some of our furniture and other long-term possessions, e.g. books.

To move home is costly, and may be an unnecessary expense at a time when our financial situation needs stability.

Any change of home must carry unforeseen risks. We may find the new home has unexpected defects, from woodworm to noisy neighbours. There may be young families with football-kicking children in nearby houses. We may find out that the piano will not fit in anywhere, that the television reception is bad and that the garden is solid clay. The climate may not suit our health. If we move to be near the children, a job move may take them away from us again.

Where to move to

Choosing the location
If a move is what we want, the choice of location will be crucial. While our main motivation (the dream, nearness to

the children, sun and sea, tax advantages, or whatever it may be) may suggest one location, long-term practical considerations may outweigh or modify it.

Practical considerations to bear in mind include such items as:

- Convenient for shops, especially food and other consumables
- Convenient for visiting with friends and family
- Good and convenient medical, dental and pharmaceutical facilities
- Good and convenient leisure activities to suit our needs and tastes
- Good public transport within and outside the area

Transport in particular is often the major problem. As time goes on, we are likely to feel less comfortable with frequent car travel. A place with good public transport may be hard to find, especially for regular journeys such as shopping. A railway station and fully-operational bus routes will be big bonuses.

A *phased* move can help to overcome the problems.
Planning well ahead offers the chance to look around. We
can visit areas we really like for weekends or holidays and
get to know them in depth. We may buy a second home in
the place we like best, and start putting down roots.
However, setting up a second home is not without danger,
especially if it is overseas. The perfect holiday spot may be
disastrous for a permanent retirement home – in many
ways, the needs of the two are quite different. Our ideal
holiday location (depending on our tastes) may be one that
offers complete peace and quiet, or perhaps an active
nightlife and plenty for young people to do. Either way, it
is unlikely to rate highly such factors as convenience for
medical facilities and regular shopping, or ease of visiting
for other members of our family. A compromise is to select
a location that will suit your retired life but is within
commuting distance, typically a seaside area with good rail
links to the town in which you work. Commuting to work
from your future retirement home in the later years of
employment may be worth facing in return for the benefits
of an established home base after retirement.

What kind of home?
The home itself will be crucially important. We will be
spending more time in it then when we were at work.
Important factors will include:

- Convenience of layout, including stairs
- Ease of cleaning
- Ease and cost of maintenance
- Heating efficiency and cost
- Size and type of garden

There is a wide choice, including:

- Houses and bungalows
- Flats and maisonettes
- Sheltered accommodation
- Living with children
- Hotels
- Campuses for retired people

Houses and bungalows

The choice of a house or bungalow for retirement living may depend largely on its garden. Unless gardening is one of the pleasures you are looking forward to, it should be small and easy to maintain. On the other hand, houses with small gardens are often close to the road, and may be noisy. Property with the fewer and smaller rooms you want may be situated in areas of young and noisy families, or in other ways be unsuitable. Finding the right age mix of the neighbourhood will be important: some prefer those with the widest mix of age-groups, including young families; for others, the empathy and quiet of people of their own age is essential.

Most houses and bungalows in the UK are freehold, without the problems associated with leases.

Flats or maisonettes

These may meet many of our objectives for retirement living. Many have a layout and size which is convenient. Most do not involve direct responsibility for a garden, even though there may be a garden available.

There are, however, a number of potential problems. Most flats are leasehold, and the provisions of leases vary and are usually heavily tilted towards the landlord. We shall not be able to take the lease, or even the interpretation of a solicitor on trust without becoming fully familiar with its provisions. Obligations for maintenance of the property itself, the general structure and the common areas (such as stairs, passages and gardens) will need study. There may be onerous restrictive covenants, even covering such aspects as the number of guests allowed to stay.

Noisy neighbours can be a serious problem in flats, especially if they are next door or overhead. The cleaning and maintenance of common areas may be a difficulty. Security may be helped by controlled access (e.g. by an Entryphone or doorkeeper), but many blocks of flats are open to all. Security will in any case be better above the ground floor.

While the landlord and the existing tenants may be responsible and cooperative when we buy, times and people can change.

Sheltered accommodation

This is now widely available. Most is restricted to residents over a specified age, often 55. A resident warden, available to help in emergency, is invariably provided.

Such facilities provide a degree of reassurance to many retired people, while not unduly restricting their feeling of independence. Some, on the other hand, may not like an exclusive environment of elderly people, and find the presence of a warden intrusive. Sheltered accommodation is always rented or leasehold, and the previous comments on leases will apply.

Living with children

This suits some families who see three generations living together as an enrichment of life and an acceptance of moral responsibility. This was the traditional view until recent times. However, many now accept that such an arrangement can cause serious problems. To have any chance of working well, separate access, bathroom and kitchen are essential.

Some larger houses have 'granny' flats or houses; self-contained flats or buildings that can be occupied by an older member of the owning family. Such an arrangement may work well, especially in the later stages of retirement, and offers continuing contact between the generations of a family, while preserving a degree of independence for all.

Hotels
If we have the resources, and particularly if we do not have a partner, we may decide to live a life of ease in a hotel. Such a lifestyle provides daily social interaction and the opportunity to meet new people of all kinds, although it can never offer privacy.

While this approach is rare, an increasing number of couples have found it attractive and financially practicable to live abroad in this way, at least for part of the year. Hotels in some holiday locations (such as Spain) offer long-term residence during the off-season at very low rates. For those seeking mild sun and a change of scene, this is an option worth considering, especially if the UK home can be let on a short lease while we are away. However, problems with the hotel service or fellow residents which may be tolerable for a couple of weeks, may drive us round the bend after six months.

Campuses for retired people
A development pioneered in the US, and recently imported into the UK, is the campus (or self-contained village) exclusively for the retired.

Such campuses have a wide range of shopping, leisure and medical facilities, and are designed to be secure and self-contained. While they are attractive to some, others would find the environment artificial and socially restricted. Costs are also likely to be higher than for other forms of retirement living. Experience with them in the UK is extremely limited.

Your own position

Partnership concerns
List the concerns you have about any aspect of your partnership, following retirement. The first section of this chapter may help to suggest areas.

Before revealing your list of concerns, ask your partner to do the same.

Compare and discuss the two lists, resolving any potential conflicts, and noting actions that will need taking.

Other family and friendships
Consider and note the effect of retirement on other family members and existing friends.

List any family and friends that you would like to get closer to after retirement. Would it help to start the process now?

Do you feel you will need to develop new friendships? If so, can you formulate any plans to do this?

Should I move home?
With your partner (if you have one), list the reasons for moving home on retirement.

List the arguments against moving home.

Which list is more powerful, and what is your final joint decision?

Where should I move to?
If you have decided to move, list possible locations, together with their advantages and disadvantages (the second section of this chapter may help). In doing so,

consider whether you have enough up-to-date information, if not, would visits help?

Is a phased move of some kind possible, and might it be helpful? If so, what steps should you take now?

If you have decided to move, what kind of home would suit you (and your partner) best?

List the criteria by which you will judge the suitability of your new home, and then rank or weight them.

Summary

- Retirement will affect our relationships with partner, other family and friends. We will need to review and work at all our relationships with care
- Reasons to consider moving home on retirement include living in a favourite location or near to children, to reduce expense, to find accommodation that is easier to run, or a better climate
- Dangers in moving home on retirement include loss of friends and neighbours, and the cost, risks and trauma of the move itself
- The criteria for choice of a new location must be realistic, and take into account the needs of ageing
- A phased move can be helpful
- Possible accommodation includes houses, bungalows, flats, maisonettes, sheltered accommodation, living with children, hotels (in the UK or abroad), and campuses for the retired

Using time (1)

Many of us only come to realise just how precious time is as retirement approaches. For this reason, we will spend two days thinking about time planning.

Today, we will look at:

- The significance of time after retirement
- The keys to success
- Back to work? Possible earning activities

The significance of time after retirement

Time suddenly takes on a different significance when we retire; unless we are prepared for the change, it can have devastating effects.

In employment, we devote about three quarters of our waking time to work. Including work-related activities (such as commuting and work travel), working lunches (not to mention working dinners and breakfasts) and the work we take home, the typical working day is about 10 to 12 hours, and for some, much more. When we retire, this abundance of prime time becomes, at a stroke, ours.

In employment, our use of time is largely out of our hands. The time we allocate to various tasks and where we carry them out is controlled by the needs of the work, or perhaps by our boss. Our working hours and annual leave are decided by our employer. In retirement, the division of most of our time is up to us. When we retire, this external control is removed.

The psychological effect on the retiree can be enormous. Like winning the Lottery jackpot, we find ourselves with no benchmarks against which to judge and control our massive new-found wealth; the scope for waste and mis-use is endless. We may feel rudderless and lost. We may invest our time, rather than our money, in crazy schemes. Parkinson's famous Law says that 'activities expand to fill the time available for their completion', and we may squander the unforgiving hours on meaningless trivia. Our response to these feelings can be crucial to the whole experience of retirement.

The keys to success

There are three keys to the successful use of time in retirement:

- Clear objective setting
- Balance between activities
- Good self-discipline

Clear objective setting
At any stage in life, good objectives give a sense of purpose, achievement and self-worth. Clear, sound objectives are crucial to happiness in retirement and we shall look at them in detail at the end of the week, when we have considered the other elements of our plan.

Balance between activities
There are so many ways in which we might spend our new wealth of time.

We may fill our day with routine. We may weed the garden and cut the lawn ever more thoroughly, devote ourselves to ever more demanding DIY activities, or keep detailed records of the weather.

We may throw our time and energy into some purposeful and demanding activity such as charitable, social or religious involvement, archeological digs, or perhaps re-opening a railway.

We may put self-development at the top of our list, taking a degree, learning to paint watercolours or to play a good game of bowls.

Especially if we are financially secure, we may decide that it's all leisure now, and make leisure activities our top priority.

We may seek to fill the void with new earning activities, whether full- or part-time (we will look at this option in detail later today).

We may let it get the better of us, and spend ever longer in bed, slumped in front of the TV, or at the bar of the local.

None of these approaches (except, perhaps, the last) can be said to be wrong in itself. But all work and no play, or all play and no work, will make Jack (and Jill) dull, tired and bad company. We may divide our time on a daily basis, a weekly pattern, or on a timetable with a degree of flexibility – whatever pattern we choose, balance is essential.

Self discipline
For many, one of the greatest advantages of retirement is that there are fewer people who can tell us what to do and when to do it, but the converse of this is that we must tell ourselves. To have, for the very first time, neither parents, teachers, nor bosses to keep us up to the mark can be scary and demanding.

The need for self-discipline is most obvious in the way we approach each day. Do we lie on in bed in the morning? Do we keep up a routine of necessary activities, or let shaving or washing up, for example, get out of hand? Do we look after the clothes we need for our various activities? Do we use a diary, and turn up for appointments on time? Do we keep up with current affairs and local news?

Back to work? Possible earning activities

Why earn?
For some in retirement the top priority seems to be continued earning, but it is worth challenging our thinking.

Continued earning may be essential. It may be the only way we can meet financial obligations, for example, a mortgage, or the education of children or grandchildren.

We may wish to continue earning to preserve a lifestyle our other income cannot support, such as expensive holidays, good food, the family home, a cottage or flat in town, perhaps.

On the other hand, we may feel we should continue earning money not because we need it, but because it has become a habit we cannot break; the way we justify our existence and preserve our identity. If this is the case, we should challenge it. A re-think may lead to a happier life.

How to earn
If you decide that earning activities must continue, there are many options. These include:

- Continuing with previous old employer
- Consultancy
- Temporary or interim employment
- New career
- Semi- or unskilled jobs
- Writing or media work
- Self-employment

Continuing with our previous employer
The practice of compulsory retirement at a specified age is virtually universal. However, most organisations have some flexibility, especially for a key employee whose skills may be particularly hard to replace. You can always float the possibility. If you are not needed full-time, there may be a part-time or special assignment opportunity.

Consultancy
Anyone can give themselves the title 'consultant'. Some do this to maintain their self-esteem after retirement. But to be meaningful, consultants must find clients for the service they can provide, which can be difficult in an overcrowded field.

Helpful steps include:

- Clarifying our area of expertise
- Marketing and selling
- Finding our USP (unique selling point)
- Collaboration
- Using our networks
- Active marketing

It will be essential to **clarify the area of expertise** in which you hope to operate. An existing reputation, published books, papers or articles will be an immense asset. If your experience and qualifications give you any choice, you will need to carry out market research, however informal, to help you choose the area of strongest unsatisfied demand.

Success as a consultant usually depends more on **marketing and selling** skills and persistence than on technical expertise. Skill in face-to-face contacts is a must. You may need to produce brochures to a high standard, undertake mailshots, telephone selling, travelling and visiting. To produce proposals and other paperwork professionally, you will need facilities for word processing, and possibly desk-top publishing.

Unless your expertise is in a clearly-defined and technical field, you will need to consider what is your **unique selling point** (commonly known as the **USP**). What will attract potential clients to use your services rather than those of others? True professionalism and excellent customer service are essential – you may need more.

A **network** of personal contacts is almost essential to success as a consultant. The more useful people you can comfortably ring up and invite for an informal chat or a lunchtime drink, the better your chances. Effective networks take years to build. The earlier you start, the better.

Many successful consultants have obtained their first assignment from former employers, and some start planning for this possibility years in advance.

Collaboration with others, preferably who are already established, can offer strength. Such an arrangement may offer a higher market profile, perceived strength, and shared selling and administration expenses. However, few established consultants are prepared to share clients or even leads with a newcomer.

Temporary or interim employment
An increasing number of agencies provide senior staff (managers and professionals) for short-term assignments they have been invited to fill. Typically these may cover sickness of a senior employee, special projects, or a period

of re-organisation, and last from a week or two to many months. One or two agencies specialise in finding openings for older people. Fees will be at a rate agreed between the employer and the agency (the agency will pay you at an agreed rate). If this option interests you, approach one of the agencies advertising or listed in appropriate reference books.

New career

Retirement may provide an opportunity to launch into a completely new career. This is usual for those in occupations where early retirement is the norm, such as the uniformed services and sportspeople.

Some have found fulfillment in roles such as teaching, social work, priesthood or media work after retiring from their first occupation. Motivation, necessary skills, persistence and contacts can bring success.

Semi- or unskilled jobs

You may be prepared to consider semi- or unskilled work. There may be local openings as cashiers in petrol stations, checkouts or shelf-filling in supermarkets, shop assistants, cleaning and domestic service, or as salespersons.

Writing or media work

Writing and media work has no age limitations. You may prefer the world of fact and write non-fiction, or the world of imagination and create fiction and poetry.

The world of **factual media work** is easier to enter. Your previous career and life to date or your enthusiasm and knowledge of a leisure interest must provide a mine of knowledge and experience that you can share with others.

The easiest way to do this is by writing articles. There will usually be a range of magazines and journals you can write for, some of which you may know of already. You can find out about others by studying newsstands and the shelves of reference libraries. For a methodical search, the annual Writers and Artists Yearbook is invaluable. You should study your target journals carefully to learn of their needs and the required style of writing.

Non-fiction books are usually written under contract. You will need to find a suitable publisher for your subject – study of bookshops and libraries and the Writers and Artists Yearbook will help. You may then make an informal enquiry, or submit a proposal outlining what you wish to write. Publishers who are interested will discuss the work further, and may then offer a contract.

Local radio stations are often open to contributions. Their culture is usually fairly informal, and a telephone discussion with an appropriate producer is the best starting point. National radio and TV are much harder nuts to crack, and best left until you have a media track record.

The market for **fiction** is difficult to enter. There are few outlets for short stories, humour or poetry; you will need to investigate carefully to find openings for the kind of material you wish to write. A number of competitions are run annually in these fields, which can provide opportunities for the lucky few.

Novel and script writing is hardest of all to break into, and needs the investment of much time and effort without any certainty of success. There are numerous literary agencies, but even to have work accepted by these is not easy.

Self-employment

Many retired people consider self-employment, for example a guesthouse, café, minicab operation, or bookshop may attract. Others may consider offering a service based on their existing skills, such as bookkeeping or a computer bureau.

Work associated with established organisations offers social contact as well as income. This can include door-to-door selling of domestic consumables, parties to sell clothing or kitchenware, or pools collection. The financial outlay involved in such work is usually low, although methods of operation, such as franchising, carry legal and financial risks.

To succeed after a lifetime in employment, we need to refocus onto a situation in which we, and we alone, bear the risks and the responsibility. Self employment in a full-time business has many snags. Probably the worst is the volume of bureaucracy and associated paperwork.

We shall have to satisfy the requirements for information of the Inland Revenue, Customs and Excise, the Health and Safety Executive, the local Authority, and the Equal Opportunities Executive. We must keep proper books. If we run a guesthouse, we shall have to cope with the Tourist Boards. These imposing bodies and many others will cause us work, irrespective of the volume of actual business we do. Few self-employed people have many hours in a week that they can call their own.

Buying an existing business needs the coolest judgement and best professional advice. The asking price often bears little relationship to its value. Leased property may present many problems. Changes in the marketplace may not be obvious to an outsider.

Finding sources of capital will need great care. Lenders such as banks will press their services on us, but need security and interest, and may foreclose. Retirement may not be the best time to risk our home or our accumulated capital.

If self-employment is a new experience, advice from disinterested sources (*not* banks or other lenders) is essential before we commit ourselves.

Your own position

Do you need to spend time earning following your retirement? If the answer is 'no', explain why this is so, as exactly as possible.

If the answer was 'yes', what is your target income for the first year?

How have you set this target?

Describe your plans to meet your income target.

What actions, if any, can you now take towards implementing your earning plans?

Summary

- The way we use time in retirement is crucial, and calls for objective setting, balance and self-discipline
- The options include household routine, charitable, social or religious involvement, self-development, leisure activities, or new earning activities (discussed tomorrow)
- Possible earning activities include continuing (full- or part-time) with our previous employer, consultancy, temporary or interim employment, a new career, semi- or unskilled jobs, writing or media work, and self-employment

Using time (2)

There are endless opportunities for the constructive use of
our time, apart from earning, and we will look at these
today. We shall consider:

- Working for others
- Self-development
- Leisure activities

Working for others

Many people regret the lack of opportunities they may
have during an employed career to help others, and may
feel that they owe a debt to a society that they would like to
re-pay.

There are many forms which such voluntary service can
take, including:

- Charity work
- Party political activities
- Public office holding
- Involvement in local causes
- Youth work
- Religious involvement
- Professional bodies

Charity work
The range of registered charities is enormous, but only a
proportion are open to voluntary help. Active involvement
can be of three kinds: organisational, operational and fund-
raising.

Organisational help may involve office holding at local or national level. Organisation structures vary, but frequently include local branches or committees, national conferences, policy-making events or campaigns.

Operational help (in providing the charity's service) is only practicable with a few charities, and may involve selection and training. Those in which it may be possible include the Samaritans, Age Concern, Victim Support and Voluntary Service Overseas (VSO).

Fund-raising is common to all charities. It takes many forms, and few will reject offers of help with these activities.

Information on voluntary organisations can be obtained from REACH (Retired Executives Action Clearing House) Tel 0171 404 0940, the National Council for Voluntary Organisations Tel 0171 636 4066, or the Volunteer Centre Tel 014427 73311.

Party political activities

Retirement provides the opportunity for those who are so minded to become involved in party politics. Such involvement may include the various activities of a party worker, local or national office-holding, and candidature, and possible election at local or parliamentary level.

'**Party workers**' are the backbone of all political parties. They participate in fund-raising, recruitment, support for meetings and other activities, and help at local and parliamentary elections.

Local party branches will have need for the usual administrative posts, such as Treasurer, Secretary and Chair. They will also have political offices, the most important of which is that of Agent, whose role is to support local Councillors, Member of Parliament or candidates, during and between elections.

Becoming a **local councillor** offers the opportunity to support both the local community and a political cause. Most parties welcome potential candidates with open arms. Councillors are unpaid, but may draw expense allowances. The council and its committees will have a regular cycle of meetings, but the time councillors spend on local issues, 'surgeries' for their constituents, and party involvement varies widely.

We may even set our sights on becoming a **Member of Parliament**. All parties have a central list of approved candidates, but the final choice will lie with the members of individual constituency parties who invariably guard this right jealously.

Public office holding

The ancient office of **Justice of the Queen's Peace (JP)**
offers the opportunity to make a major contribution to the
local community.

The duties involve regular attendance on the bench of their
local magistrates' court (typically about a morning a week).
In addition, JPs are frequently requested to sign official
documents (e.g. passport applications), and may be called
on for special sittings or other duties. Training is given,
especially in the early stages.

Any citizen may apply, through the local Clerk to the
Justices, to be considered for appointment as a JP. There
has been a tendency in recent years to choose younger
candidates, but if you have taken this up while still
working, you will be able to devote more time to it on
retirement. The process involves interview and vetting
before being listed. After listing, appointment can only be
made when a vacancy on the appropriate Bench occurs.

Such offices as **college governor** and membership of a
district health authority offer scope to those with
appropriate interests and skills. While a proportion of such

posts are filled by those already holding certain positions (e.g. members of staff, trade unionists, local councillors), there are also openings for the general public.

At national level, there is a large number of public bodies, boards, committees and commissions often called **quangos (quasi autonymous national-governmental organisation)**. You may have suitable contacts through your professional association, political party, trade union or personal network. If not, it is open to anyone to ask that their name should be placed on the national register of those called upon for such duties – the 'Great and Good'.

Involvement in local causes
Some people feel strongly about specific local causes and issues, and retirement may provide the opportunity to devote time and energy to pursuing them. These may include such issues as local road building (for or against), the closing of local hospitals or schools, maintenance of law and order, pollution, or local facilities generally.

Effective action will need the support of others. We may pursue them through one of the main political parties, through membership of the Parish Council (if we have one), a Residents' Association, or an Action Group dedicated to the issue. However we decide to act, such commitment often proves to be demanding of time and energy, even of money, and desperately frustrating. The forces of bureaucracy and vested interests are strong, and can draw on immense resources (most of which we pay for). We may also, besides making friends and allies, find we have made enemies.

Youth work
Recent discussion of child abuse has tended to put many adults off youth work. However, the need for responsible

adults to become involved in youth activities such as the Scouts and Guides will always remain. Many youth organisations, such as the Church Army and the Crusaders Union, are attached to religious bodies or centred around religious beliefs.

Religious involvement
Retirement offers the opportunity to devote time to the many religious activities which always need the support of those with appropriate beliefs.

Churches, chapels, temples, synagogues and other religious centres all offer a range of opportunities for active involvement. Typical are those of the Church of England, which includes such offices as membership of the Parochial Church Council (and higher, national lay bodies), sidesman and lay preacher.

For those of deep religious conviction, there are institutions offering the opportunity of full-time membership, possibly involving residence in a community.

Professional bodies

Many retired people find satisfaction in helping the work of their professional institution. Involvement may help us to keep in touch with ex colleagues, and contribute to the development of our profession. Such bodies invariably need the help of their interested members both at local and national level. Many have local branches with regular meetings and are controlled by committees of members. At national level, there will be an elected council or similar body, usually supported by committees, panels or working parties.

Self-Development

New skills, new interests, new friendships and new experiences can only add to our satisfactions and achievements at every stage of our life. Because our circumstances will change as we age, so the need for new, appropriate interests and activities is always present. In particular, as the body ages, so it becomes even more important to develop our mind and keep it active.

Qualifications

We may decide to obtain new qualifications. At degree level, the Open University (Tel 01908 653791) and Open College (Tel 0161 434 0007) offer distance learning courses (i.e. courses that can largely be followed at home), and require no pre-qualifications. If we already have appropriate qualifications, courses at other universities may be open to us: if we have a first degree, we may decide to obtain a master's, or perhaps a doctorate. University courses can be full- or part-time, with distance learning elements.

Information on current courses can first be obtained from directories available in most reference libraries; full information can be obtained from the institutions themselves.

Local colleges offer a full range of courses leading to certificates and diplomas in virtually any subject. A glance through the prospectus can be a revelation. National organisations include: the National Institute of Adult Continuing Education (Tel 01533 551451) and the Workers' Educational Association (Tel 0171 402 5608).

Other courses
Courses that do not lead to qualifications are widely available. They can be of almost any length, and cover almost any subject; they can be during the day, evening, weekend, summer school, residential days, weeks or months – the variety is endless.

We do not need to attend classes to develop systematically. Distance learning courses (what were once called 'correspondence courses', but now often include tape or computer-based material) are widely available. A visit to a good public library will set us on the track of both local and national opportunities.

Other development
There is no need to go on a course – you may decide to undertake your own study, and develop through appropriate reading and other learning activities. There are also unlimited fields for original research, any of which may be within your interests and resources. For some retirement has provided the chance to develop expertise and reputation at national level.

Leisure activities

The capacity for simple enjoyment is all-too-often blunted during our employed life. Retirement offers a glorious opportunity to re-awaken this vital faculty.

Leisure activities can replace the working companionship we have lost, keep us fit in mind and body, help to rebuild our partnership, and strengthen new and existing friendships – but more than anything, they can be fun!

As we said yesterday, balance in our post-retirement activities is important. Among other factors, this balance should take account of the seasons; for instance golf in the snow is not much fun.

The types of leisure activity include:

- Sport and physical activities
- Artistic and craft activities
- Reading
- Indoor games
- Domestic activities
- Travel
- Other interests of all kinds

Sport and physical activities

Sport is best played for enjoyment, not as a duty. We shall look tomorrow at health in retirement, of which exercise must be an element.

Our active days in the sports of our youth (rugger, soccer, hockey or whatever) will be over long before retirement; we now watch our team rather than play in it. But our contribution as referee, umpire, linesman or coach may be invaluable – to us and to the club.

There are also many sporting and physical activities we may continue to enjoy, or even take up for the first time. Our game of squash, tennis or badminton may not be as fast as it was, but it may be more cunning. Some cricketers have played into their sixties. The long list of other possibilities includes aerobics, archery, bowls, cycling, dancing, sailing, swimming and walking.

Artistic and craft activities
Retirement may at last allow us to satisfy our interest and develop our skill in some artistic or craft activity. This may make an ideal winter complement for the outdoor activities of summer. There are clubs and classes everywhere waiting to welcome us, and books in every bookshop to put us on the right path. The choices are endless, including: drawing, embroidery, knitting, model-making, music (playing and listening by going out to concerts or at home), painting, pottery, rug-making, singing, the theatre (attending performances, or taking part in amateur dramatics from acting to make-up), and woodwork.

Reading
Retirement will give us the time to read for pure pleasure – to explore new authors and revisit old favourites. We can also read about new subjects as an element in self-development.

Indoor games
Television has driven many to forget the delights of indoor games. Some, such as chess and bridge, can be played at any level of skill – at home, in clubs, by computer, or even (for chess) by post. The endless variety of card games stretches from patience to gin rummy, and snap to poker.

Domestic activities

Home-based activities are a favourite with many retired people. While they do not get us out and about, they can be highly satisfying, and are sometimes a necessity. They offer scope for experiment and perhaps development of special knowledge and skills. Gardeners may start growing their own vegetables; cooks may enhance their dinner parties with new-found skills in Indonesian cuisine; DIY enthusiasts may learn to plaster a ceiling.

Travel

Some retired people have the urge to see new parts of the world, visit friends or family abroad, or just get away from the UK weather. Others explore their native country, maybe for the first time, perhaps visiting castles, country houses and historic sights.

Many forms of special interest travel are now available, both within the UK and overseas. These include trips to follow a touring sports team (e.g. the English cricket team in Australia) or to special events (e.g. the Olympic Games); study tours and cruises, complete with lectures from experts; and walking, cycling and sailing holidays at various levels of skill and experience.

Other interests of all kinds

There is, of course, no limit to the new or long-held interests we may choose to follow in retirement. For all there will be, if we want them, appropriate clubs or societies. Here are a few, from the thousands available: antique collecting, archeology, astronomy, ballooning, canoeing, darts, family history, fell-walking, fishing, flying, gliding, local history, orienteering, parachuting, parascending, photography, scuba diving, stamp collecting, railway restoration, skiing, water-skiing, wine-making, and yoga.

Perhaps the danger, after all, is to try to do too much.

Your own position

List retirement activities that you feel would interest you (and your partner, if you have one). Use the headings in this chapter: 'Working for others', 'Self-development' and 'Leisure activities'.

Review the list carefully, asking:

- Which activities from this list are my top priorities (no more than three or four activities)?
- What time, energy, interest and other resources will each priority activity require? Will I have these?

- Will these priority activities clash with any earning activities I am planning? If so, how can the clash be resolved?
- Do the priority activities match well together, and provide a balanced mix for achievement, enjoyment, mind and body?

Produce a final, revised list of the priority activities you plan to undertake in retirement.

Summary

- Opportunities to spend time working for others include charity work (whether organisational, operational or fund-raising), party political activities (including local counsellor), public office holding, involvement in local causes and issues, youth work, religious involvement and involvement within professional bodies
- Self-development opportunities include obtaining formal qualifications at every level, non-qualifying courses, distance learning and self-controlled study or research
- Leisure activities include sport, artistic and craft activities, reading, indoor games, domestic activities, travel, and many others, most of which are supported by clubs, societies or other organisations

Fitness and health

As we grow older, health and fitness may become a more conscious pre-occupation. Retirement both generates the need and offers the opportunity for a thorough review. Today, we will look at the subject from several angles:

- What are 'fitness' and 'health'?
- Mental attitude
- Exercise
- Diet

Our relationship with our GP (general medical practitioner) becomes progressively more important as we age. We should feel able to consult our GP for advice on any health-related matter. If you do not get on well with your doctor, you should do something about it: try getting to know him or her better, and if this fails, transfer quickly to another.

What are 'fitness' and 'health'?

Fit for what?
The word *fit* begs the question 'Fit for what?' To be fit to run a marathon or play a game of rugger is one thing; to be fit to dig our garden, or walk to the station is another. We should not assess ourselves against inappropriate standards. The sensible question is: 'Am I fit for the kind of life I wish, and might realistically expect, to lead?' We should also ask: 'How realistic is my expectation?' Although the rate of ageing varies, no-one can turn the clock back. Our expectations must not be based on wishful thinking.

We can think of such fitness in terms of the bodily systems required: strength of the necessary muscles, lung capacity, digestion, heart and circulation, eye-sight, hearing, etc.

General health
There is an obvious link between fitness and general health. Fitness will help us to fight disease and perhaps to avoid it. Exercise and diet help to guard against some common illnesses, such as heart disease. General fitness also creates a literal 'feel-good' factor, which contributes to mental and physical health. Abuse of our bodies by eating unwisely, use of drugs, excessive alcohol, exposure to the sun, or physical strain, increases our liability to illness.

The accepted belief is that we should be fit for our normal lifestyle, but also to have a reasonable reserve. How much reserve is 'reasonable' is a decision we alone can take, if necessary, with professional advice.

What seems to be the problem?
If we feel unfit for the life we wish to (or must) lead, it is sensible to find out why, and unless the causes are obvious, we should seek professional advice.

Many health conditions, including some of the most life-threatening, can be cured if diagnosed early enough. We will need to be alert (without becoming hypochondriacs) to possible signs of conditions associated with ageing, such as male prostate troubles; female breast cancer; and for both sexes, cancer of the digestive tract and heart troubles.

Regular and thorough medical check-ups can give some people a peace of mind, although a few find the check-ups a source of anxiety (they are available through a number of medical insurance groups, but if you do not belong to one of these, your GP will be able to advise you).

We should also always get advice before making major changes in our lifesyle (such as by undertaking exercise programmes) or making changes to our basic diet (such as by slimming or becoming a vegetarian).

Getting (or keeping) fit
Having decided that we are in good general health and that our fitness expectations are reasonable, we can plan a programme of controlled maintenance or improvement. This will usually be based on exercise, diet and our general lifestyle. We will think in detail about these subjects in the following sections.

We may need artificial help to meet our expectations. Fitness for driving, in particular, is crucial for many lifestyles. We need regular sight tests and may have to wear glasses as we get older. Regular dental examination is also important. Deterioration in hearing can be checked and discreet hearing aids worn if necessary.

Mental attitude

Healthy bodies and healthy minds tend to go together. Just as physical problems can lead to depression and other psychological difficulties, so stress and other psychological problems can affect almost any bodily function.

The effects of retirement
The link between body and mind is of particular importance at retirement, for several reasons. Psychologically, we may lose our sense of security, identity and purpose, and the

society of our colleagues. Physically, our eating habits, amount of exercise and sleep patterns may change. The association between retirement and ageing may raise, perhaps for the first time, fears of physical deterioration and death.

The positive approach to retirement planning we have followed throughout this week will help to minimise these problems, but they cannot be entirely eradicated. As with all concerns, it is wiser to face these fears directly rather than let them fester beneath the surface.

Stress
We may feel that escape from stress, is one of the biggest advantages of retirement. However, retirement may bring new causes of stress, such as financial worries, isolation, or partnership difficulties. For a few people, the absence of stress itself causes stress; they find it difficult to wind down. We have looked at each of these causes of stress during the week – if they remain a problem, it may be wise to seek professional advice.

Hypochondria
Obsession with our state of health may become a problem in itself. Other consequences apart, this makes us insufferable bores. Few enjoy visiting the doctor, but he (or she) is the one person to whom we should talk freely about our health concerns.

This five-stage plan may help those with this tendency:

1 Evaluate our symptoms as objectively as possible.
2 Seek advice promptly if it seems necessary.
3 Act, if required, according the advice we have been given.

4 Shut up lest we become a chronic bore.
5 Forget - unless further symptoms indicate we
   should run round the loop again.

Common problem areas
Three areas in particular may cause worry as age creeps up
on us: sex, sleep and fading memory.

Our physical relationship with our partner can change as
we get older. Some see this as a blessing, others find it hard
to accept. Difficulties can sometimes be helped by
treatment and it is always worth seeking advice.

A good night's sleep is essential to mental and physical
health. What constitutes a 'good night' varies widely
between individuals, but most require less as they age. We
may go to bed later, and wake up more frequently during
the night and earlier in the morning. This is only a
problem if it starts to worry us.

Dependence on alcoholic nightcaps is generally frowned on,
and sleeping pills are now far less frequently prescribed.
Some advise a warm, milky drink last thing or not going to
bed until 'sleepy tired'; others advise reading in bed until
you are tired, but there is little general agreement. As with
other concerns, a chat with our GP may help.

Fading memory is another effect of ageing which can be
both inconvenient and embarassing. Here are some
suggestions to lessen its effects:

- Keep notes, especially of telephone discussions
- Keep a methodical appointment diary or calendar

- Repeat and use the names of people we meet as frequently as possible
- Exercise the memory, preferably in an enjoyable activity such as indoor games or competitions (many retired people have successfully entered Mastermind)

Memory loss concerns some as a possible symptom of Alzheimer's Disease. It is unlikely, in isolation, to be a symptom. The best course for those with doubts is to seek early professional advice.

Exercise

Suitable, regular exercise helps to maintain general health and fitness, but opinions about the best amount vary. The UK official guidelines currently recommend three half-hour periods a week of brisk walking or the equivalent.

Exercise can be obtained in several ways, separately or in combination:

- General lifestyle
- Participation in sports and games
- Individual exercise programmes
- Health clubs and sports centres

General lifestyle
If we spend most of our time in front of a computer or TV screen, extra exercise will be a must. If, on the other hand, we cultivate a large garden or walk daily to the station or the nearest village, we may have little need for additional exercise. Combining exercise with necessary routine is ideal.

Participation in sports and games
Regular participation in sport or games can be a satisfactory and enjoyable method of all-round exercise: if it is still practicable for us, it may be our first choice. We explored such possibilities yesterday.

Individual exercise programmes
Walking, cycling, swimming and 'jogging' are regarded as good all-round exercise. Various forms of home exercise equipment (such as exercise bicycles) are available; these are not affected by weather or traffic conditions. A cheaper and satisfactory method is to follow an exercise progamme which can be completed at home without any extra equipment, such as that for Canadian Airforce Personnel (published by Penguin).

Health clubs and sports centres

If we seek the body beautiful, balanced muscular structure and the flattest stomach we can manage, a complete and balanced programme will be necessary. Health clubs, fitness and sports centres have equipment, facilities and (in most cases) expert advice to help. Health clubs may be expensive, and offer little that is not available far more cheaply from our local sports centre. Many sports centres offer exercise programmes and classes specially designed for older people.

'Health farms' may appeal, offering residential facilities with integrated programmes of exercise, diet, and other elements such as massage or bathing. They are often expensive, and are regarded by some as more of an occasional treat than a serious contribution to long-term health.

■ F R I D A Y ■

Diet

A healthy diet

Good diet is agreed to be essential in maintaining good health. Unfortunately, frequent changes and disagreements between experts, and fears about the influence of vested interests, has produced cynicism.

Despite these doubts, there is much common ground. Most agree that over-eating in itself is damaging, and that the amount of food of all kinds necessary to maintain good health reduces with age. It is accepted that a healthy diet should include plenty of fresh fruit and vegetables. There is general agreement that a high intake of fat, especially saturated fat, is harmful.

Alcohol

The UK government has recently increased its recommended maximum weekly intake of alcohol to 28 units for a male and 21 for a female. One unit is a normal-sized glass of wine, fortified wine or spirits or half a print of beer, lager or cider. There is now fairly general acceptance that a moderate intake is beneficial – certainly of red wine. Beyond this, unless we suffer from specific conditions in which alcohol is harmful, we must make up our own mind.

Dietary supplements

Vitamin, mineral and similar pills and potions have had a varied press. The general medical view is that a balanced diet makes them unnecessary. There are also doubts as to the extent to which the body is able to take in and use them. However there is a substantial volume of users who are prepared to attest to their value, and some research to support this view. Again, the decision must be ours.

Obesity

Many older people become concerned about 'middle-age spread'. Diet and exercise should hold this in check, but some feel the need for slimming programmes or foods. The long-term value of such efforts has often been queried. If obesity concerns us, a chat with our GP is likely to be more useful than bottles of the latest slimming compound.

Smoking

The harmful effects of smoking are now generally accepted.

Your own position

Health

Have you any concerns about your present health? If so, what are they? (Be totally honest!)

What action have you taken about each of the concerns you have listed? Do you honestly believe it is appropriate and adequate? If you have received advice from qualified medical practitioners (including use of medication, changes to diet, drinking habits or other aspects of lifestyle) are you following it?

If you have not consulted a qualified practitioner about these concerns, why not, and should you not do so?

Exercise

What exercise do you now get, week, by week?

Do you consider this is adequate and appropriate for your needs? If not, plan necessary changes, seeking qualified advice if you have any doubts whatever.

Get on with it!

Diet and drinking habits

Do you consider you have a healthy and balanced diet and good drinking habits, taking into account the best current advice of which you are aware?

If not, what changes should you make? Why have you not made them?

Get on with the changes!

Summary

- The relationship between patient and General Practitioner becomes more important as we age
- We must be clear about what standard of 'fitness' is appropriate for us
- We should be alert, without becoming hypochondriacs, to any symptoms of ill-health; regular check-ups can be valuable
- Psychological well-being is as important as physical health. Stress can cause problems even in retirement. Common problem areas during ageing include sex, sleep and memory
- An appropriate amount of regular exercise is valuable. It can be obtained through general lifestyle, participation in sports and games, individual exercise programmes, or use of health clubs or sports centres
- A generally healthy but not faddy diet is an aid to health and fitness. Alcohol intake should be controlled. Dietary supplements may help

Piecing it all together

We have spent this week looking at each aspect of retirement, and considering our own situation. Today, we will piece the elements together. We will consider:

- When to leave
- Retirement objectives
- The action plan
- As the day draws near

When to leave

Retirement can be thrust upon us by our employer, perhaps with the shortest of notice. But this risk should not deter us from looking at retirement proactively, and asking:

- What flexibility do I have over the date of my retirement?
- When should I retire?

What flexibility do I have over the date of my retirement?
The concept of flexible retirement ages, to meet the needs
and circumstances of individual employees and employers,
is widely acccepted in theory, but very rarely in practice.
However, we should be aware of how much flexibility, if
any, we may have.

Many people would prefer a phased run-down, and a few
employers offer their employees the choice to move from
full- to part-time work. Others may offer work to retired
employees on a self-employed or consultancy basis, or
retain them for specific projects. Some people view
retirement with horror, and would like to continue in full-
time employment. It is always worth discussing
possibilities with our employer as retirement age
approaches.

We should be familiar with the rules of our occupational
pension scheme, the normal retirement age, and the effect
of early or late retirement. If we have a private pension, we
must ensure we know the conditions attached to it, and its
likely value.

The self-employed may stop working at whatever age suits
them – provided their customers still have work for them
to do!.

When should I retire?
Of course, we might decide to quit our job at any time and
follow a life of our own choosing, but this happy option is
not realistic for most of us. The date of our retirement will
depend on factors outside, or only partly within, our
control. Nevertheless, retirement can usually be sensibly
considered at any time between the ages of 50 and 65.

It is helpful, therefore, to start considering our decision soon after reaching our mid 40s. The sooner we form objectives and plans, the more chance we will have of achieving them. Our decision may affect our present lifestyle and require time to implement: we may need to save hard, to obtain fresh qualifications, or to start putting down roots in a new location. Clear retirement objectives and plans will also give a sense of security and purpose as our career moves towards its close.

In considering when to go, the most important factor is usually the conditions of our pension provision. Heavy 'actuarial reductions' are levied against early retirers, and we will need accurate information about our own situation. We shall also need to bear in mind any gap before we receive a State Pension, and the possible need to continue voluntary contributions to obtain maximum entitlement.

Other questions that will affect our decision include:

- How much do I enjoy my current occupation, and what prospects does it offer?
- Are there other interests or activities I seriously wish to pursue? If so, when would it become too late to do so?
- What are my present family responsibilities, and how are they likely to change in the foreseeable future?
- How healthy am I and how healthy is my close family?
- What are my occupational, personal and state pension expectations?

- What other sources of non-employment income do I
  have, and how much would it be? Consider interest
  on capital, insurance policies maturing, annuities,
  property rents, and so on

Retirement objectives

The value of objectives
We have touched on the importance of clear objectives
several times during the week (some people prefer to call
them 'targets' or 'aims'). Objectives help us set priorities
and make decisions. They help us to make the best use of
time. They give the psychological security that comes from
knowing where we want to go. Achieving them will give
us great satisfaction.

During employment, our objectives are thrust upon us by
other people and by the needs of our work; in retirement,
we must set our own. We will have more freedom to
control our lives than ever before: we must use it to the
full!.

Good objectives
Good objectives should be:

- Clearly thought through and worded
- Challenging
- Realistic and attainable
- Measurable, or at least possible to check
- Consistent with each other

Setting our retirement objectives
We can set our first list of retirement objectives at any time
(as we have already suggested) the longer in advance of
retirement we start, the more help they will be.

If we have a partner or other members of the family who
will be affected, it is essential that they should work with
us on both objective setting and planning.

Once made, objectives can be reviewed at intervals to
ensure they are still valid and to make any necessary
changes, both before and after retirement. We may do this
annually at the turn of the year, instead of New Year
Resolutions, or perhaps on our birthday. We should also
review the objectives if there are any major changes in our
circumstances, for example redundancy, unexpected
promotion or job change, loss of a partner, serious health or
financial problems. As time goes on, we will need to add
new objectives to replace those we have achieved, or to
meet new aspirations or interests.

Our list of objectives may not be long and should not be
unduly complicated, but it should cover all the main
aspects we have touched on during the week:

* Finance
* Family and relationships
* Residence
* Use of time
* Health and fitness

The stages of objective setting are as follows.

1 Look back over this book, and the answers you have given to the 'Your Own Position' questions at the end of each chapter.
2 'Brainstorm' possible objectives (jot down as many as possible, quickly and without criticising).
3 When ideas have finally run out, review the list carefully: clarifying, removing duplications and overlaps, eliminating the unimportant or mistaken, and adding any that are missing.
4 Re-write the list in priority order.

John Nokes is now 53, and has decided to retire on his 60th birthday on 5 April 2001, when his full occupational pension will become payable. Here are his retirement objectives:

JOHN NOKE'S RETIREMENT OBJECTIVES

(made jointly with Mary Nokes)

Version 1: 5th April 1996

- To live in a two-bedroom flat, house or bungalow in Southwold
- To maintain my present capital resources intact for use either to provide long-term care for Mary or myself, or if not so used, to pass to our children
- To develop and practise my skills as a painter of oil-colour landscapes, if possible to exhibition standard
- To complete climbing of all peaks listed in the Wainwright guides to the Lake District
- To become an active member of the Suffolk Branch of the Institution of Information Technology, and an office holder at branch and national level
- To join and be an active member of the appropriate branch of Victim Support
- With Mary, to visit one new country each year

The action plan

The pieces are now in place for us to produce a retirement plan. Our objectives state *what* we will do and the plan *how* we will do it. It must indicate:

- The actions to be taken
- The timescale on which each must be taken
- Who (if not us) must act
- The resources needed for each

John Nokes is lucky to have sufficient capital to buy a residence in Southwold as a second home. Here is his Retirement Plan, based on the list of his objectives that we have seen.

Action	Started by	Finished by	Who acts	Resources needed
Choose & buy Southwold home	Now	1/1/2000	M & J	Up to £75,000
Sell present house	5/4/2001	ASAP	J	From sale
Save more capital	Now	5/4/2001	J	As much as as possible
Furnish Southwold home	When bought	5/4/2001	M & J	£2,000 + from present home
Dispose of surplus furniture, etc	1/1/2000	when house sold	M & J	None
Become active in local IIT branch	Now	Now	J	Time only
Join Victim Support	Now	Now	J	Time only
Join painting class	1/9/1999	1/9/1999	J	Time only
Keep up hill walking fitness & skills	Now	5/4/2001	M & J	Time only

It is worth noting how many activities John should start straight away, seven years before he plans to retire.

Our planning will need periodic review. It will become more detailed as activities start. It may need revision if deadlines are missed or obstacles encountered. Those who are familiar with network planning may feel it is worth setting up a network for any critical activities, such as a move of home.

As the day draws near

The long-awaited day is now approaching fast. Hopefully our preparation and planning has ensured that we await its arrival with calm confidence, if not excitement. It is to be the first day of a new and fulfilling period of our life.

The actual process of retirement from an organisation may cause some anxiety.

Final check on our pension entitlement
If we will be eligible for a State pension, we should have received a proforma about four months in advance from the local office of the Benefits Agency asking for certain information including our choice of payment method, and this should be followed within about a month by a statement of our entitlement. If these do not arrive, we should contact the Agency's local office.

The Personnel Department (or our boss if there is not one in our workplace) should help in the weeks beforehand to ensure that arrangements for our occupational pension have been made. Depending on the provisions of the scheme, we may need to choose between a lump sum and additional pension. We should also ensure as early as possible that we know exactly what the starting amount will be and when and how it will be paid.

Income tax
If the local office of the Inland Revenue are aware of our retirement (e.g. through our previous tax return) they should send a form asking for up-to-date information on our financial position, and expectations of income following retirement. If they do not do this, we should contact them and explain the position. After receipt, they should issue a fresh tax code, and we may be entitled to a refund of tax.

The leaving ceremony
Most organisations make some ceremony of retirement. It is common practice to present a card and a gift from colleagues. Depending on custom and practice, we may be asked to choose the gift in advance, and a little preparatory

thought will make this easier. There is also the likelihood of being expected to make a speech of thanks after the presentation. Some people feel this as an embarrassment, and keep it as short as possible. However short and simple, we should mention:

- Our appreciation of any gift
- Our thanks for any kind remarks made during the presentation
- Our sorrow at leaving our colleagues, and the hope of maintaining contact
- Our best wishes to all for the future

If we feel up to it, we may take the opportunity to make a rather fuller speech – it is, after all, a once-in-a-lifetime event. If we do, we may piece together something including such elements as:

- Our first memories of the organisation
- Salient, and especially humorous episodes over the years
- The major changes we have seen
- The support we have received from our closest colleagues
- Our own plans in retirement (but not too much about them)

It is usually best to ensure we have a chauffeur to hand to ensure a safe journey home; from then on, life is ours to live – happy retirement!

Summary

- We should establish what flexibility, if any, we have over the timing of our retirement
- If we have a choice, we should consider the best timing of our retirement at the earliest opportunity
- Retirement planning should begin by setting, well in advance, clearly defined objectives
- An Action Plan, based on our objectives, should be produced well in advance; these should indicate the necessary actions, when they should start and finish, who must carry them out, and the resources they require
- The Action Plan should be revised and updated as necessary
- A few months before retirement, we should carry out final checks on our pension position and any other key factors
- We should be prepared for leaving presents and parties